EXCAVATORS & DIGGERS

Super Explorers

Excavators & Diggers

What Are Excavators & Diggers?

Excavators and diggers are powerful machines. They are some of the biggest machines on Earth.

They work on construction sites and in mines. They also dig tunnels.

Excavators and diggers can dig large holes and even knock down buildings. They also carry away dirt and rocks.

Some machines have wheels and others have tracks. The wheels have huge tires. Sometimes the tires are taller than a person. The tires have ridges to help them grip the ground.

Wheels and Tracks

Large wheels and tracks let the machines go over rough ground. Excavators and diggers can go almost anywhere!

Tracks are wide, metal belts. They have ridges that let the machine travel on muddy ground. The tracks also keep it from sinking into soft ground.

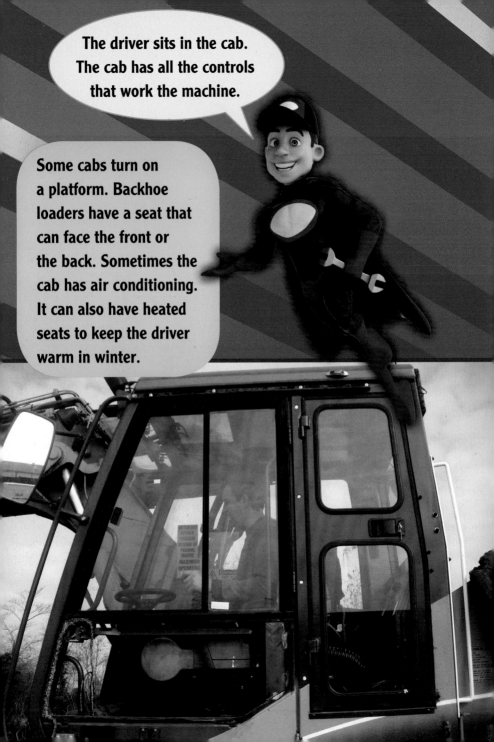

The driver sits in the cab. The cab has all the controls that work the machine.

Some cabs turn on a platform. Backhoe loaders have a seat that can face the front or the back. Sometimes the cab has air conditioning. It can also have heated seats to keep the driver warm in winter.

The Cab

The cab has windows all around to let the driver see in all directions. They keep out dust and rain.

Controls

The driver works the controls in the cab. Each kind of control does something different.

Colour

Excavators and diggers are usually painted in bright colours. They are often yellow, orange or red.

The bright colours make the machines easy to see. This is important when many machines are working on a construction site.

Yellow and orange also mean caution. Be careful around big machines!

A backhoe has a bucket at the end of a long arm. The arm has a joint in the middle, like an elbow. The arm moves up and down. It can also move sideways. It stretches out so the bucket can dig.

Backhoe

Backhoes have stabilizer legs. The legs keep the backhoe from tipping over while it is working.

The backhoe digs by pulling dirt backwards. When the bucket is full of dirt, the arm lifts it up.

A front-end loader looks like a tractor with a big, wide bucket on the front.

A loader cannot dig down into the ground like a backhoe. The bucket scoops up dirt, sand or gravel.

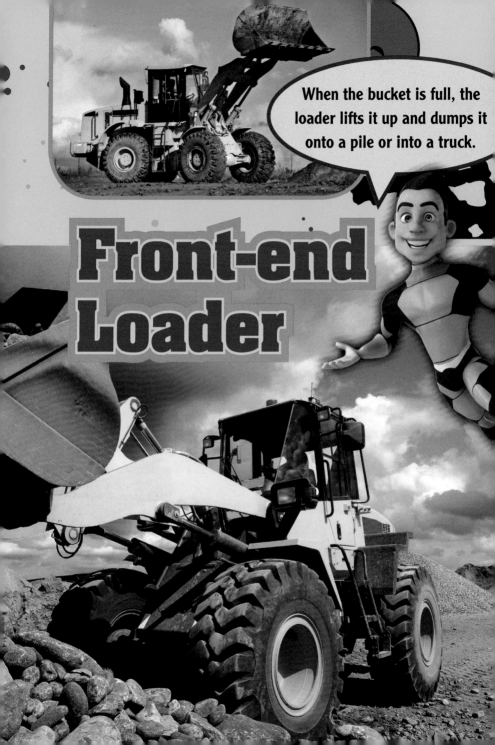

When the bucket is full, the loader lifts it up and dumps it onto a pile or into a truck.

Front-end Loader

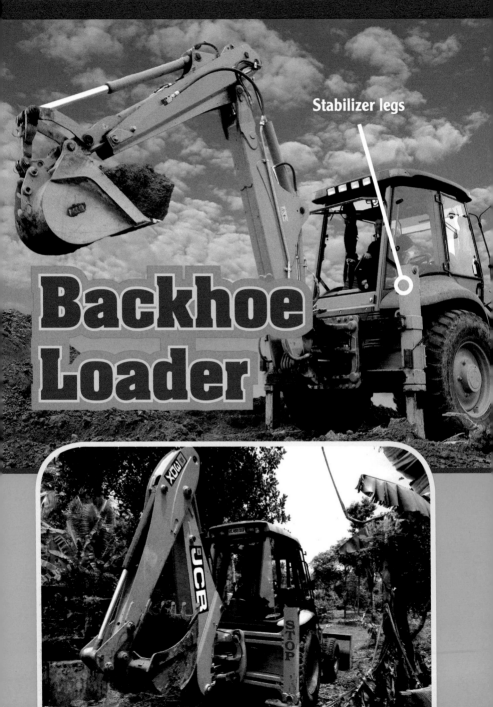

This machine is a front-end loader with a backhoe.

Stabilizer legs

Backhoe Loader

Blade

The blade on the back is called a ripper. It looks like a big claw. It breaks the ground so the other machines can take the dirt and rocks away

Bulldozer

Graders are mostly used in road construction. They make a wide, flat surface for the asphalt. Graders are also used to remove snow from roads in winter.

Grader

A grader has a long, metal blade. The blade scrapes off the top layer of soil. It makes the ground flat.

Some graders are so big that they have two motors. One motor drives the front wheels. The other motor drives the back wheels.

Excavator

An excavator looks like a backhoe but it has tracks instead of wheels. It has a long arm with a bucket for digging.

The word "amphibious" means that the machine can work on water and on land. It can only go in water that isn't very deep.

Pontoons help the excavator stay above the water. They are like big, steel balloons. The tracks go around the pontoons to help the machine move forward.

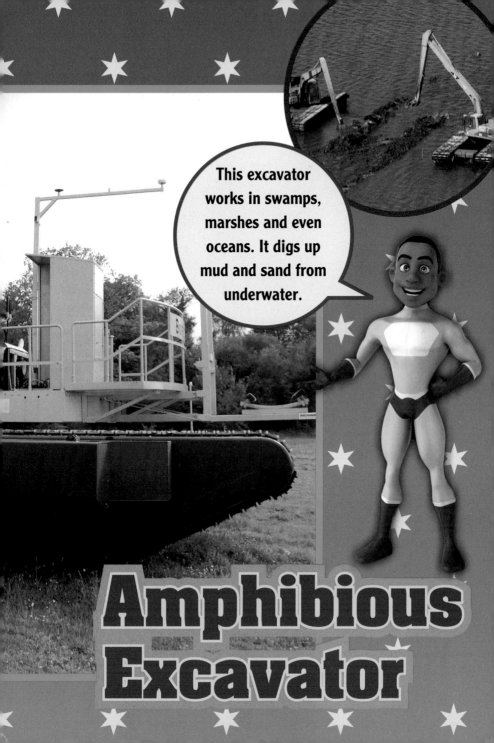

Amphibious Excavator

Tunnel Borer

This mega machine has a giant cutting wheel with many teeth. Some teeth cut hard rock or chew through soft dirt. Other teeth remove the dirt and rock.

A dredger is a machine that excavates mud and sand from the bottom of lakes, rivers and harbours.

Dredger

A dragline has a big bucket attached to a long arm called a "boom." Wire ropes and chains control the bucket.

Boom

Bucket

Draglines are some of the biggest excavating machines in the world. They are used in coal mining and in oil sands.

Dragline

The operator drops the bucket, then drags it across the ground.
When the bucket is full, the boom lifts it up. Then the boom
swings around and the operator dumps the bucket.

The teeth also take dirt and rock out of the trench. The trencher moves forward very slowly as it cuts. The operator controls how deep the cut is.

Trencher

This excavator has a giant wheel with scoops or buckets. The buckets pick up dirt and rocks. They put the dirt and rocks on a moving belt that takes them away.

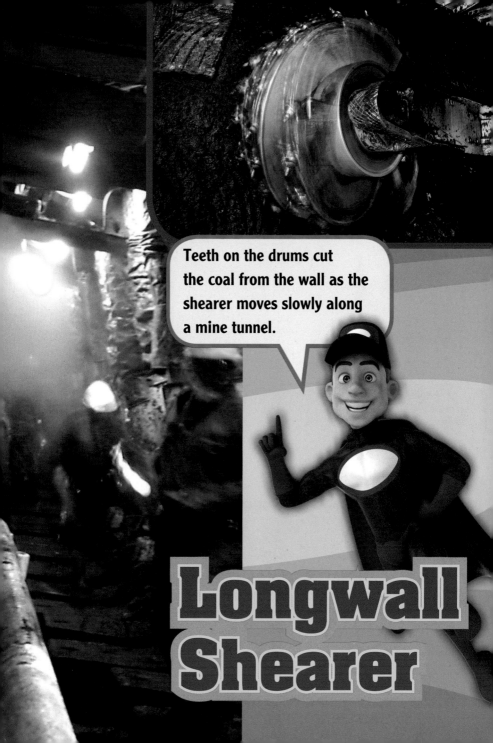

Teeth on the drums cut the coal from the wall as the shearer moves slowly along a mine tunnel.

Longwall Shearer

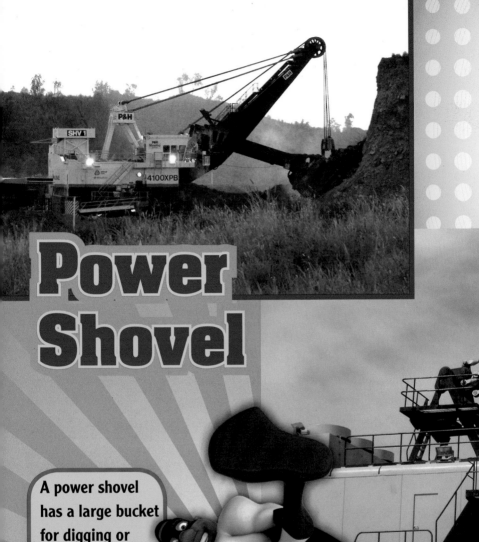

Power Shovel

A power shovel has a large bucket for digging or excavating. The bucket is at the end of a long arm called a "dipper."

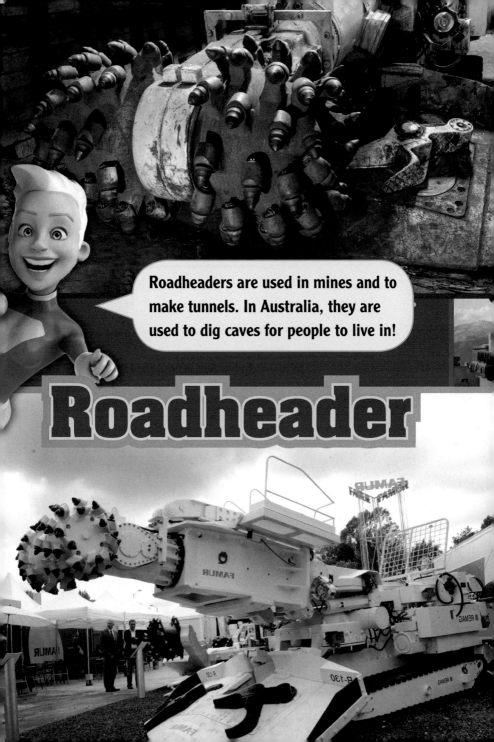

Roadheaders are used in mines and to make tunnels. In Australia, they are used to dig caves for people to live in!

Roadheader

The cutting head can be a cone or a ball. It has teeth or spikes. The head turns, and the teeth cut through the dirt and rock.

A roadheader has a cutting head on the end of a long arm. Some have two heads.

Not all drills go straight down. Some drills can go sideways. This is called "horizontal drilling." A horizontal drill is often used to install underground pipes or cables.

It can drill under roads or waterways. This drill doesn't disturb anything on the surface.

Horizontal Drill

A hydraulic shovel looks a lot like an excavator. It has a bucket at the end of a long arm. It also has a cab that turns.

The shovel arm is wide and thick. It is very strong. It can lift very heavy loads. The large bucket has teeth. The teeth help the bucket scrape up rocks and dirt.

Hydraulic Shovel

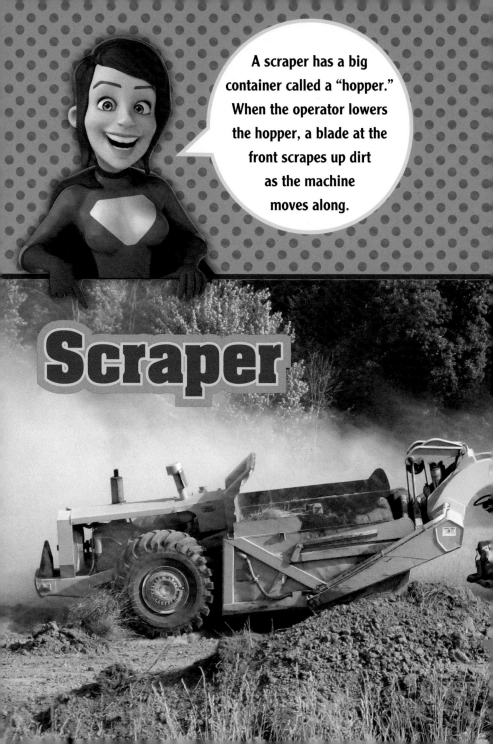

A scraper has a big container called a "hopper." When the operator lowers the hopper, a blade at the front scrapes up dirt as the machine moves along.

Scraper

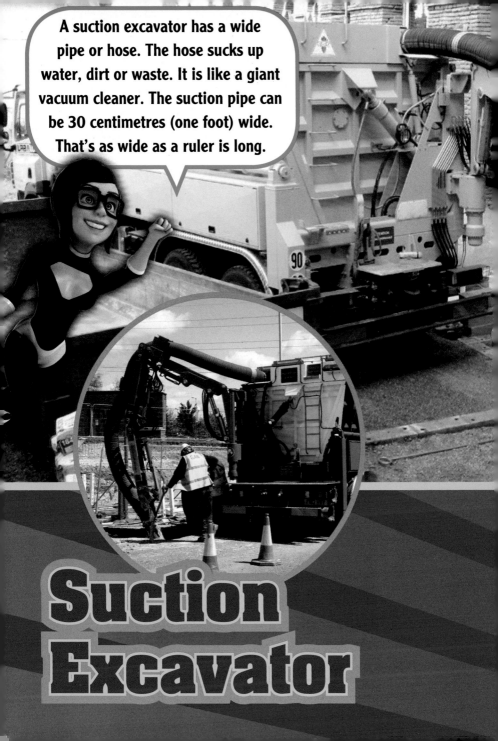

A suction excavator has a wide pipe or hose. The hose sucks up water, dirt or waste. It is like a giant vacuum cleaner. The suction pipe can be 30 centimetres (one foot) wide. That's as wide as a ruler is long.

Suction Excavator

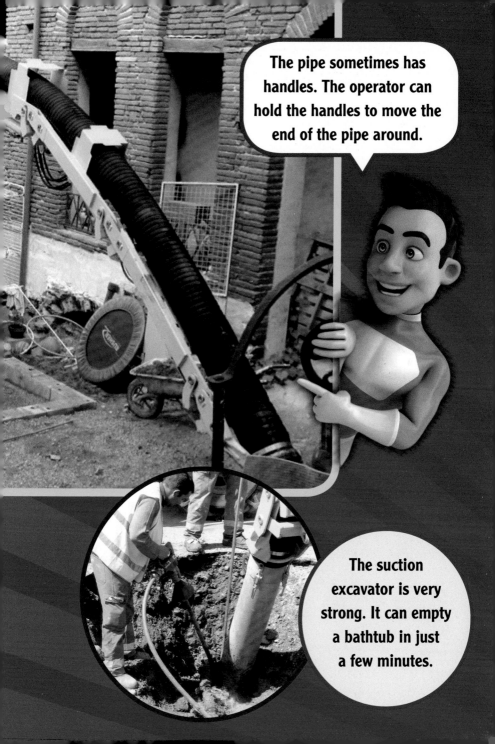

Highwall Miner

The highwall miner is used in coal mines. It has a cutting head with many teeth. When the head spins, the teeth cut the coal.

A claw crane has a long arm called a "boom." The operator can make the boom longer or shorter. At the end of the boom is a grabbing claw. The operator can raise and lower the claw.

Hydraulic Breaker

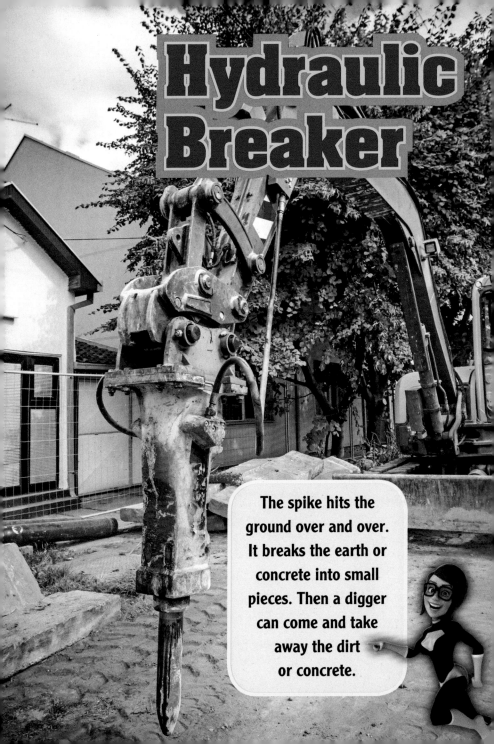

The spike hits the ground over and over. It breaks the earth or concrete into small pieces. Then a digger can come and take away the dirt or concrete.

The world's largest land machine is the Takraf Bagger 293. It is a bucket-wheel excavator. It is as long as 7 football fields. It weighs more than 30 jumbo jets.

World's Largest Machine

It takes five people to operate the Bagger 293. This excavator is used in coal mining.

More Biggest Machines

Front-end Loader

The world's largest front-end loader is the Le Tourneau 2350. It can lift 65 tonnes (72 tons). That's the same weight as 15 pickup trucks.

Superdozer

The Komatsu D575A-3 is the world's largest bulldozer. This superdozer is used in construction and mining.

Tunnel Borer

The Herrenknecht S534 tunnel borer is the world's largest tunnelling machine. It makes tunnels for roads and railways. It can make tunnels up to 16 metres (50 feet) high. That's as tall as a four-storey building.

Hydraulic Shovel

The world's largest hydraulic shovel is the Terex/Bucyrus RH400. It is used in the oil sands. It can lift 85 tonnes (94 tons). That's as much as 17 elephants.

Even More Biggest Machines

The Publisher: Mega Machines is an imprint of Blue Bike Books

Library and Archives Canada Cataloguing in Publication

Excavators & diggers / Super Heroes.
(Mega machines)
Issued in print and electronic formats.
ISBN 978-1-926700-65-6 (paperback).
ISBN 978-1-926700-67-0 (pdf)

1. Excavating machinery—Juvenile literature. I. Super Heroes (Children's author), author II. Title: Excavators and diggers.

TA735.E93 2016   j621.8'65   C2016-901107-0
                                           C2016-901108-9

Front cover credits: Front end loader, FourOaks/Thinkstock; super heroes, julos/Thinkstock.

Back cover credits: Herrenknecht S534 tunnel borer, sochi/Flickr; Terex RH400 shovel, gongkong/Flickr; Bucket wheel excavator, thyssenkrupp/Flickr

Photo Credits: Every effort has been made to accurately credit the sources of photographs and illustrations. Any errors or omissions should be reported directly to the publisher for correction in future editions. *From Flickr:* cab outside_Flickr, 6; inside cab_Flickr, 7; Doosan, 9; Floating Plant Services, 24; secondavenuesagas, 26; BRoseke, 27; crisc, 39; Famur, 40; i2mine, 41; Kevin Land, 50; Earthmovers, 60; gigantesdomundo, 61; borer_sochi, 62; gongkong, 63. *From Thinkstock:* Mr_Twister, 2; Zoonar RF, 3; snvv, 3; Pi-Lens, 5; SCHUBphoto, 5; RGtimeline, 7; Gennady Kravitsky, 10; _Pilin_Petunyia, 11; rodho, 11; outsiderzone, 12; CBCK-christine, 12; SLampkin USAF, 13; LUHUANFENG, 14; FourOaks, 15; Dmitry Kalinovsky, 16; Jupiterimages, 17; thepoo, 18; Dmitry Kalinovsky, 19; apichat_naweewong, 21; Tuayai, 21; Jupiterimages, 23; Jupiterimages, 23; Decent-Exposure-Photograpy, 28; scalatore1959, 29; tolstnev, 29; DMitri Melnik, 30; Kerry Werry, 31; der Naut, 34; meliusphotography, 36; Jacek_Sopotnicki, 37; EunikaSopotnicka, 40; drill_garth11, 42; Achim Prill, 46; apinunrin, 46; Achim Prill, 47; _Dan Dumitru Comaniciu, 54, 55; Joe Gough_, 55; roman-23, 56; roman023, 57. *From Wikipedia:* EC160E-excavator, 8; Hans Haase, 8; Lone Star Kenya, 15; Ramesh NG, 16; MathKnight, 18; Tano4595, 20; Ccolem02, 22; Jean Housen, 24; Steve Hillebrand_USFWS, 25; Luminant_Energy_Kosse, 30; Diablokrom, 32; Tesmec SpA, 32; Ditch Witch, 33; UN Navy, 33; Eickhoff Engine Works and Iron Foundry, 36; Sansumaria, 38; Ingolfson, 43; Dwight Burdett, 44; FRAC, 44; Syracuse Utilities, 45; DangApricot, 48; Bill Jacobus, 49; Mickael Lucas, 51; DSpindler, 52; CMMC, 53.Background Graphics: IgorZakowski/Thinkstock, 2, 3, 6, 23, 35, 38, 58, 63; shelma1/Thinkstock, 4, 21, 40, 44, 55; NoraVector/Thinkstock, 10, 41, 45; Lana_Stem/Thinkstock, 13, 53, 56; kennykiernan/Thinkstock, 15, 43; Daniel Rodriguez Quintana/Thinkstock, 18, 26, 56; DavidGrigg/Thinkstock, 24, 28, 31, 46.

Background Graphics: IgorZakowski/Thinkstock, 2, 3, 6, 23, 35, 38, 58, 63; shelma1/Thinkstock, 4, 21, 40, 44, 55; NoraVector/Thinkstock, 10, 41, 45; Lana_Stem/Thinkstock, 13, 53, 56; kennykiernan/Thinkstock, 15, 43; Daniel Rodriguez Quintana/Thinkstock, 18, 26, 56; DavidGrigg/Thinkstock, 24, 28, 31, 46.

Superhero Illustrations: julos/Thinkstock.

Produced with the assistance of the Government of Alberta, Alberta Media Fund.

Alberta Government

We acknowledge the financial support of the Government of Canada through the Canada Book Fund for our publishing activities.

Funded by the Government of Canada
Financé par le gouvernement du Canada | **Canada**

PC: 35